Praise fo

"This close encounter with the shimmering soul of poet and visual artist Leslie Neustadt will leave each fortunate reader with the taste of honey soaked challah in their mouths and stark visions of the sojourn of this girl-becoming-woman in a world cluttered with voices of her elders, of the men who took her power and the raging beauty of her reclamation. The poems will leave the reader's skin touched by silk and tenderness, hearts pumping with vivid memories tempered by gorgeous prayers for the future. 'Draw signposts upon your body to mark your way,' the poet writes in her grandmother's voice. Readers may suckle at the breast of this Kali spirited author, who with fierce tongue and ceaseless response meets both transformation and sorrow with equal grace. This collection itself stands as a signpost for readers to guide them through the many transitions life brings. Eloquent and elegant, these poems nourish the reader hungry for soul satisfaction."

Suzi Banks Baum, artist, mother, author and editor of
An Anthology of Babes: 36 Women Give Motherhood a Voice

"An autobiography in poetry…a life that has borne fruit year after year, finding richness and nourishment in soil that has weathered droughts, high winds and earth shattering quakes. Having buried much and many during her journey, she pauses, turns back, dares to unearth the bones and offers them to us so that we may see and know. Raw and real and fearless. A reader must simply say thank you."

Molly Bloom, MFT, artist and psychotherapist

"The 72 poems that appear in Leslie Neustadt's *Bearing Fruit* are braided like challah, the Sabbath bread which represents the manna given to the ancestors during their long years of wandering. From the beginning of this remarkable collection in which the author journeys into her personal and ancestral past, the reader becomes a spellbound traveling companion, seeking to assemble the configuration of secrets that lay just under the storied surface with the clues clearly revealed. There are many unexpected gifts in careful reading of Leslie's poetry. But make no mistake: these poems transverse beyond nostalgia in order to find redemption in what is real. Using archetypes, astronomy, hip hop, gastronomy, mathematics, and shamanic dance, Leslie accomplishes a feat of God-wrestling, as she becomes both the one who carries her past in her troubled bones, and the one whose words become our own very healing balm."

Yael Flusberg, author of *The Last of My Village*

"Leslie Neustadt's title poem *Bearing Fruit* begins: 'Sometimes truth / has sharp edges / that pierce my skin.' These lines express a raw intimacy, an unflinching language that reaches out to me throughout this book. Neustadt bears witness to the dark and light experiences which are an integral part of her human and her soul story. Her poems startle me to feeling and, at times, they soothe. Despite the wrenching experiences she has endured, she holds a deep capacity for recognizing truth and beauty."

John Fox, author of *Poetic Medicine: The Healing Art of Poem-Making*

"Leslie Neustadt is a gift. Her raw-boned, unvarnished humanity and quest for forgiveness—of both herself and others—resonate throughout the journey on which she takes us. Her poems, at once delicate and compelling, teach us to 'surrender shame' and 'sense true north' in the unmapped territories of our lives. 'Death's startling kiss' has indeed honed her vision, so that each poem sings with a quiet insight insisting on being heard. Through moving us deep into her life, these poems move us deeper into our own."

Natalie Reid, author of *The Spiritual Alchemist: Working with the Voice of Your Soul*

"Leslie Neustadt's poetry will move you to both laughter and tears. Her authentic voice and amazing insight will carry you to a deeper understanding of her personal journey and your own life. With brave and razor sharp insight, this powerful poet writes of a life fully examined. Her words both sing and sting. Timothy Green stated in *Rattle* #38, 'Poems say what cannot be said another way: they construct new worlds in response to the confines of this one...and leave you feeling changed.' *Bearing Fruit* will leave you 'feeling changed.'"

Linda Leedy Schneider, LSMW, writing teacher, mentor and psychotherapist and author of *Some Days: Poetry of a Psychotherapist*

"Neustadt's personal narrative intersects with social and cultural events taking the reader on a sensate journey from the Civil Rights Movement through modern rap music. Honest about suffering and early abuse, mortality and joy — *'the messy stew of life'*— these poems arrive at a devotion to beauty, finding it in the language of names, *'Seagalit, my purple peanut,'* the Dalai Lama and *'the lotus of his laughter,'* and in knowledge that keeps us *'close to the earth.'*"

Myra Shapiro, author of *12 Floors Above the Earth* and *Four Sublets: Becoming a Poet in New York*

A Poetic Journey
by Leslie B. Neustadt

With the author's gratitude to Judith Prest, Publisher
Spirit Wind Books, P.O. Box 15, Duanesburg, NY 12056

© 2014 by Leslie B. Neustadt
Trade paperback ISBN: 978-0-9666891-9-8

Front cover mixed media artwork, *Woman Dancing with Joy*, by Leslie B. Neustadt.
This work incorporates the stamped image of a face titled *Woman in Repose* ©2005 by
Suzanne Nicoll. Used with permission of the artist.

Cover and author photos by Joan Heffler.

Book & cover design by Deb Tremper, SixPennyGraphics.com.

For further information and permissions approval or to order copies of this book, go to
www.LeslieNeustadt.com

First Edition, 2014

Printed in the United States of America

Dedication

To the memory of my beloved sister, Laurie Ellen Neustadt,
and the circles of women who helped me find my voice.

Ye shall know them by their fruits. —MATTHEW 7:16

Preface

I came to writing late in life. Most of my adult years were spent practicing law and raising my two sons. It was only after life broke me open that I was ready to write, and then only in circles of women who opened their hearts to my stories. Writing has become an affirmation that my life has meaning and has helped me uncover gifts in the challenges life has presented me. As Naomi Rachel Remen has written, "Our poetry allows us to remember that our integrity is not in our body; that despite our physical limitations, our suffering and our fears, there is something in us that is not touched, something shining. Our poetry is its voice."[1]

Many people helped me bring this book to fruition. I would never have begun to write without Marilyn Day. She invited me to join her peer writing group, womanwords. With her encouragement, I began to attend the International Women's Writing Guild, where I found wonderful teachers and mentors, including Anya Achtenberg, June Gould, Dorothy Randall Gray, Yael Flusberg, Marge Hahn, Jan Lawry, Jan Phillips, Natalie Reid, Linda Leedy Schneider, Myra Shapiro, and Susan Tibergian, among others. I began to work with Linda Leedy Schneider in 2005. This book would not have been written nor published without Linda's encouragement, compassion, wisdom and unerring instinct for editing poetry. I have also been privileged to study with Barbara Ungar. My work has benefited from the feedback provided by her, as well as the students and participants in her classes and workshops. I have flourished with the nourishment I receive from the Women Writers and Artists Matrix founded by Amejo Amyot and Dorothy Randall Gray. I am also

---

1   Remen, Rachel Naomi, M.D. Preface. *Poetic Medicine: The Healing Art of Poem-Making.* By John Fox. New York: Jeremy P. Tarcher/Putnam, a member of Penguin Putnam Inc, 1997. xiii-xiv. Print.

grateful to have worked with John Fox, the Director of the Institute of Poetic Medicine, who introduced me to the therapeutic nature of writing and sharing poetry in a supportive environment. The Hudson Valley Writers Guild has provided support and inspiration and a venue for me to share my work.

I am grateful to the women with whom I have written and shared my writing, including Amejo Amyot, Kittie Coffey Bintz, Judy Clough, Marilyn Day, Kelly de la Rocha, Trish Ford, Mary McCarthy, Judith Prest, Rosette Rubins, Lesley Tabor, Angela Thomas, and Dolores Wilson, among many others.

Barbara Delage of Springboard Literary has been invaluable in submitting my work for publication, advising me about self-publishing and promoting my work. She oversaw every aspect of this book during the publication process. Rachel Moritz reviewed and proofread the manuscript, winnowed down the poems and suggested how to order them and, in so doing, shaped the arc of the book. The book's graphic design and formatting were artfully handled by Deb Tremper of Six Penny Graphics. I am most grateful to Suzi Banks Baum, Molly Bloom, Yael Flusberg, John Fox, Natalie Reid, Linda Leedy Schneider, and Myra Shapiro, for graciously agreeing to review *Bearing Fruit* and liking the book well enough to endorse it. Molly Bloom rescued the artwork for the cover from a dust heap of my old collages. Joan Heffler photographed me as well as the artwork for the cover. My husband, Gary, has provided loving support throughout my transformation from a practicing attorney to a woman who pursues the healing art of self-expression in a variety of forms. My sons, Matthew and Benjamin, my daughter-in-law, Mary Beth, and my grandson, Mason, have given joy and purpose to my life.

I am blessed to have an incredible extended family and friends who sustain me in a myriad of ways. I am deeply grateful for their love, encouragement and inspiration. And I would not be here without a dedicated and compassionate team of health care providers and healers who have kept me alive, sometimes in spite of myself.

For every copy of this book sold, the entire purchase price of *Bearing Fruit* will be shared among not-for-profits that benefit patients with amyloidosis and/or Waldenström's macroglobulinemia, aid children who have been abused, or use expressive arts as a healing modality.

Acknowledgments

These poems have appeared in slightly different form or under different titles in the following publications:

Akros Review: "*Segalit*"

The Bloomsbury Anthology of Jewish American Poetry: "The First to Go"

Cure Magazine (on-line): "The Waiting Room"

Jewish Women's Literary Annual: "Triangle of Unfinished Business"

Mentor's Bouquet: "Teshuvah," "Thank You, Tupac"

Found Poetry Review: "Listen"

Mused: BellaOnline Literary Review: "Around the Corner," "A Triangle of Unfinished Business"

Poetica Magazine: "The First to Go," "Mishmash"

Veils, Halos and Shackles, International Poetry on the Abuse and Oppression of Women (forthcoming anthology): "*Teshuvah*," "Carry-On Baggage," and "Unspeakable"

Workers Write, Tales from the Courtroom: "May It Please the Court"

Table of Contents

I

Mishmash. 3

I Am Still Hungry for the Old Country 4

The First to Go 5

It's What I Didn't Say That Haunts Me. 6

Namesake. 8

Upriver 10

Avinu Malkeinu, Our Father, Our King. 11

Blessed Bones. 12

Segalit 13

The Remains of the Day. 15

Our Stories Were Never the Same 16

Braided Lives. 17

After 30 Years 18

Dance of Deathlessness 19

To Go To Transylvania. 22

II

Invisible Star 27

A Triangle of Unfinished Business. 28

Where Were We? 29

What Happened to *Shana Leah?*. 30

Brush with Madness, Circa 1970 31

Unspeakable 32

Teshuvah 33

Reparations 34

Carry-On Baggage 35

What If? 36

Perversed Pleasure 37

Confessions of a Sugar Addict 38

You Don't Understand 39

I Can't Forget His Brown Alligator Shoes 40

Bad Boy of Neurobiology .41

I Did Not Set Out to Be Cruel 42

May It Please the Court 43

First-born 45

Thank You, Tupac 46

The Sacrament of Sushi 47

Bitter Greens 49

The Salt Wars, Circa 2010 .51

Water Is My Temple 52

III

Resurrection 55

Turning Point 56

Child of My Child 57

After My Husband Has Seen 25 Patients 58

Blood Offering 59

The Waiting Room 60

Listen, Please Listen 61

Death's Seduction 62

Around the Corner 63

Stringing Beads at Gilda's Club 64

The Cartographer 65

Night Sounds, Circa 2003 66

Thank You 67

Memento Mori 68

Lunar Eclipse. 69

IV

A Remembrance of Beauty 73

Sandhogs 74

Reflection. 75

Under Cover of Night. 76

Listen 77

It Must Be Hard to Be an Icon. 78

Nestled in the Shade of the Elder Tree 79

Beads of Wonder. 80

Recurrence 81

Waiting Room II: The Amyloid Clinic 82

Immersion 83

Silence. 84

Awash with Images. 85

Piece by Piece. 86

I Want to Live 87

Forgiveness. 88

Symphony of Blues 89

Flower of a Thousand Petals 90

Aftermath. 91

The Seed Keepers 92

Bearing Fruit 93

I

Remembering is the source of redemption.
—Ba'al Shem Tov

Mishmash

I come from small town Amerika
with a *schmear* of *Yiddishkeit*.
Grandma Frieda and Grandpa Charlie
spoke *mama loshen*, mother's tongue,
and Greenhorn English.
Forced into sweat-shops
on the lower East Side,
they never taught us to sew.
Our fingers were meant to turn pages.
Every Friday night, we lit *Shabbos* candles,
ate roast chicken and *challah*,
prayed at Temple Beth-El.
Grandma Frieda would save our places.
She planted a red kiss on my cheek
as I snuggled by to sit
among aunts, uncles and cousins.

I belonged to that Tinkelman clan.
Still long for that Tinkelman clan.

I'm a mishmash.
Flavored with Grandma Frieda's
chicken soup, I floated
in her fragrant brew,
sucked the *feecelah* of young hens.
Wrapped in endearments of people
long gone, I can still hear
Ziese, sheyna madelach, Lesincoo, Leslele.

I Am Still Hungry for the Old Country

For delicacies first dreamed
in Romania and Russia,
born of need, nothing thrown away.
Brains, hearts, lungs, livers, tongues,
tendered and sauced, sweet and sour.
Food stuffed into viscera and skin,
stitched by hand with white thread.
Helzel, flour flavored with fat,
squeezed into the skin of a chicken's neck.
Kishka, carrot and onion stuffing
forced into a cow's intestines.
Chicken livers and onions fried
in *smaltz*, fed into the meat grinder.
Live carp kept in a cast-iron bathub,
ground into gefilte fish.
Noodle *kugel* bound by an alchemy
of cow's milk, creamed with butter and sugar.
Strudel perfumed with cinnamon and apples.
Huzen Bluzen, dough crisped with confectioner's sugar.
If only I could taste these delicacies again.
Drink a *glayzele* of mint tea, sugar cube in my teeth,
surrounded by my grandparents.

THE FIRST TO GO

Over 50 percent of Jewish young adults marry outside their faith.

The edges were the first to go,
the fenced yards that defined us,
the cut glass bowls that contained us.
It was only later that the sacred chants,
the velvet scrolls were forgotten.
What once was sweet and rich
as the garnet wine we sanctified
thinned to a bittersweet brew.
We still hear faint psalms floating to heaven,
remember dipping braided bread
in wild honey and sage.
Our ancestors' exhortation, *dor l'dor*,
generation to generation,
a guilty secret tattooed on our wrists.
We watch some born of our seed
walk toward the horizon,
welcome the freedom,
the unclouded sky.

It's What I Didn't Say That Haunts Me

Think of something you said. Now write what you wish you had said. —William Stafford

I.

Blacks and whites gathered
to face racism
after the Million Man March.
Panelists, a facilitator,
microphones for the audience,
the illusion of civil discourse.
I didn't mention being Jewish.
Instead I explored the invisible
privilege of white skin.
But another panelist asked,
*What about you people
and the Nation of Islam?
They're anti-Semitic.*
From the audience, a minister
from the Nation of Islam
leapt up, two bodyguards at his side.
He catalogued Jewish sins,
cast us as children of Satan,
his rhetoric a terrifying sing-song.
I sat mute in the face of his fury.
No one else stood up to his rant.
Afterwards, a Jewish man
approached me, screaming,
Shame on you! Shame on you! Shame on you!

6

II.

When the minister sat down,
I wished I had stood up,
moved to the center of the stage,
turned to the facilitator and asked,
Why didn't you stop that litany of hatred?
Does one person's suffering give him
a right to heap venom upon another?
I am no preacher. No ringing
cadence springs from my lips.
But this I know.
Casting an entire people in sin is wrong.
We need to stand up against prejudice,
no matter who is the object of scorn.

Namesake

To Leah Glotzer, *my great-grandmother*

What treasure I discovered in Kiev where you grew up—
not the Pale of Settlement where most Jews were forced
to live. I never imagined that your husband made fine
cabinets for royalty. I thought you huddled in steerage
with your *landsmen*. Instead, you shared a porthole with
your husband and seven children, paid with silver secreted
in the hem of your Persian lamb coat.

But once you passed through Ellis Island, you joined the
wretched on the Lower East Side. Your older daughters,
once dowried, were parceled out to sweatshops. Your
husband stared out the dirty window, listened to the din of
street hawkers, too depressed to work again.

Great Grandma Leah, why didn't I know you turned your
three-room flat into a lunch room for factory workers?
Your little ones peeled potatoes and onions while you
ground gefilte fish from carp swimming in your bathtub,
your kitchen fragrant with roast chicken, kugel and
cabbage borscht.

Without your story, how was I to understand my Grandma
Frieda? She never lost her regal bearing and turned Grandpa
Charlie from a button-hole maker into a dress manufacturer.
Grandma painted on brown eyebrows, tinted her hair
blue until the day she died. How was I to understand her

pride in her skinny blue-veined legs, her stout body and ample bosom? She refused to teach her children to sew and struggled to send her three sons and daughter to college during the Depression.

How was I to understand my mother, Norma? Grandma wrapped her only daughter in satin, made sure her soft hands were never pricked by a needle, saved, Grandma Frieda thought, from suffering.

Upriver

After laboring in sweat shops,
my grandparents made
their way upriver
to open a dress factory,
Poughkeepsie good
as any non-union town.
My father wholesaled
candy and tobacco.
We worked hard,
dressed well,
noshed on sweets.
No Jews allowed
in the Golf and Tennis Club,
so we created a man-made lake,
established a Jewish Center.
But we couldn't live
on Jewish food alone.
I still craved
straight blond hair,
slim thighs, a pert nose.
I wrapped my coarse
hair around Coke cans,
scotch-taped my bangs,
had my hair straightened
until it fell out.
Bald, four-eyed,
braced and chubby,
I found no escape.

Avinu Malkeinu, Our Father, Our King

There are days I cannot stop
chanting the *Avinu Malkeinu,*
the solemn prayer we sing on *Kol Nidre,*
the holiest night of the year.
We beseech *Avinu, sh'ma kolenu, hear our voice.*
We confess, seek mercy, pray,
write us in the in Book of Life.
I cannot carry the tune
or remember all the words.
I no longer believe
Avinu determines my fate.
But when I chant the *Avinu Malkeinu,*
I feel Grandpa beside me,
dressed in a crisp white shirt,
with its starched promise
that our sins will be washed away.
I see Rabbi Zimet prostrate
himself before the Holy of Holies,
importuning *Avinu* to show us mercy.
I hear the choir chant the plaintive tune.
When the mournful pleas of *Avinu Malkeinu*
seep into my soul, the sacred chant sings me.

BLESSED BONES

Blessed are the bones of the beloved,
though the marrow has seeped away.
Bleached white they lie uncovered,
their remains revealed in riverbed.
No longer bearing cruelties inflicted,
holy relics of cherished days.
Blessed are the dreams of the beloved,
though they never saw the light of day.

SEGALIT

My breasts ached,
swollen with milk
for my daughter
whose life was so brief
there was no time to nurse her.
So tiny and purple,
inflamed from sepsis
that seeped into my womb.
A dream nurtured
over the seven months
I carried her.
She lay in my arms,
too weak to suckle,
until she breathed no more.
After three miscarriages,
I trusted my mothering
time had come.
Allowed myself to love her fully
as she squirmed in my belly.
In the end, sour milk
hardened in breasts
that yearned to nourish her.
My rabbi intoned,
Your daughter did not live
long enough to be named.
No shiva or kaddish required.
My husband laid her
to rest in an unmarked grave

between his grandparents.
There she remains.
Pain smoldered in my breasts
until my friend said, *just name her.*
Segalit, my purple peanut.

The Remains of the Day

Three weeks after my sister's death,
her married lover stripped
her apartment bare.
He left us a few cardboard boxes—
family letters, a few mementos,
some drawings, her diaphragm,
her ashes in a black plastic box.
He had taken leave of his life
to care for her. Upon her death,
he took what he wanted and left.
To Laurie Ellen, Jonathon was
the Sufi poet of her dreams.
We saw his dark shadow.
We unpacked those cardboard
boxes as if they were filled with gold.

Our Stories Were Never the Same

We shared paper dolls, twirled
in blue tutus, savored sundaes,
chased fireflies at dusk. But
our stories were never the same.
No matter our intention,
there were things left unsaid.
No matter what our mother
told us, some wounds do not heal.
We chose to bury the tangled
skein of our sisterhood.
It wasn't until you lay dying
that I joined hands with your
Sufi sisters and learned
the Dances of Universal Peace.
Fourteen years have passed
since I washed your body,
brushed your tangled hair,
wiped you clean for the last time.
I imagine you beside me.
The scent of orange and ginger
fill the room. I want to believe
that you would choose me
as your sister again.

BRAIDED LIVES

For Shelley Kolin

Our lives are braided like challah,
its sacred yeast redolent
with family traditions
handed down *l'dor v'dor*,
generation to generation.
She asks, *froggie, what's up?*
My hunger abates nourished
by love that birthed us both.
Once again we are *Lesincoo* and *Shelala*,
endearments echo in shared veins.
We polish the tarnished silver,
set the table with blue and gold porcelain,
raise Grandma Frieda's rose-colored glasses,
and dine on challah and honey.

After 30 Years

We sit around the alabaster table
after our *Seder.*
Porcelain platters carry *matzoh,*
the bread of affliction.
My brothers and I
finally lift the shroud.
We gently defrock our mother,
sainted these 30 years.
We overthrow the pharaoh of fear,
divine her life from the bones of memory.
Once four, we three
are left to ask the questions.
We seek the true measure of this woman,
dead for more than half our lives.
This time we weave her life
from whole cloth.
No records of his rage remain,
but the shadow of our father darkens the frame.
Though she did not protect us,
we needed her a saint.
Like a star magnolia, she bloomed briefly,
a fragile, creamy love.
We reclaim what is real,
rewrap her in silken cloth.

DANCE OF DEATHLESSNESS

*The Merina tribe of Madagascar practices the custom of
Famadihana. Extended families gather at their burial
grounds, remove their ancestors from the tombs, dress them
in new shrouds and dance with their bones.*

Moonlight leads me to the stone temple.
I open the ossuary doors, dress
the earthen goddesses who begot
me in new shrouds of silk.
I sit at their stony feet,
dance with their silvery bones,
divine wisdom from their dust.
I lift up my baby girl and my sister
like the Torah, sift through their ashy sand.
Sing their gossamer tales—a song of songs.

Great Grandma Leah
My namesake. Mother of seven,
married to the Tsar's cabinet maker.
You left Kiev to come to the *Golda
Medina.* Then parceled out your children
to sweat shops, opened your
kitchen door to factory workers.
What do your tired bones have to tell me?
Great Grandma Leah warns,
*Learn to quickstep through quicksand.
Jump into the fire of change.*

Grandma Frieda

Sturdy boned, despite skinny legs
marked with rivers of blue,
you bridged old world and new.
I was sweetened on your sugar cookies.
Do you still draw on your brows
with a brown pencil on the other side?
Grandma Frieda intones,
Draw signposts upon your body
to mark your way.

Grandma Jeannette

Are you still wearing the chiffon frock
you made to waltz with your "gentleman caller"
just after Grandpa Hugo died?
Does your chest bone heave
from the pain your son sowed?
Grandma Jeannette replies,
Dance away your tears. Don't lay your father's sins
at my feet. He was his own invention.

Mommy

Thirty-seven years in the ground.
I am ten years older
than you were when you died.
I wear your worry beads
around my neck. Have
your bones found the peace
that eluded you when you
tread the earth?

My mother sings,
Shana madelach, my sunshine girl,
let your worry beads fall away.

Laurie Ellen
Beloved sister, I can't dance with your bones.
You chose fire over decay.
Over a decade dead, you left me
divining rods to find my way,
as if you knew the filmy passage
before you made the *hadje.*
Laurie Ellen chants,
Sing with the cinerous. Surrender to the sea.
There is no such thing as the Everlasting Pea.

Segalit
My barely born daughter.
I never saw your final nest.
Tiny as a marabou
without its downy feathers.
I gather your tender bones,
shroud you in my arms.
What lullaby do you sing?
Segalit whispers,
Sweet mama, find another to shelter in your arms.
Let others shelter you.

I behold their creamy bones.
Trace the scrimshaw of their dreams.
Swirl until their whitened sticks
sing a Song of Songs.

To Go To Transylvania

After Adam Zagajewski's *To Go to Lvov*

To go to Transylvania I must take the first stop
in Judapesto to visit the Witch of Portobello
at dusk so she can cast a spell.
Only then will I be able to forge my way
through the Carpathian mountains,
have Dracula lead me to Bram's Castle
on the other side of the forest,
at moon-night, where trees stand guard,
their needles sharp as spears,
and foxes, red as rubies, peer
from behind the pinebush.
Gray wolves howl, and the dead roam free.
Poor Transylvania, caught
between the Ottomans and the Habsburg,
the Romanians and the Hungarians,
the Russians and the Germans.
A breeding ground for blind love
for the motherland, whomever she may be.
Transylvania had golden moments
sweet as truffled honey,
but the writing on the Citadel foretold the end.
The magnificent Dohany Synagogue
sprang from the earth, sent
Hebrew chants to heaven.
But there is no ignoring the Jewish Question.
Hasidic dynasties were born in Transylvania

in the face of massacres, forced baptisms,
days when soldiers cut beards and *pais*.
So I pack and leave hastily for Transylvania
decades too late to find
the remnants of my family home.
Grandpa Hugo and his seven siblings
couldn't have known that I would try
to resurrect them. They fled Transylvania
before Jews were forced to wear yellow badges.
There once was too much Transylvania.
Now it no longer exists.
Still I seek to understand
how its cruel mountains,
the dark hallways of its green forests,
the vampires, the burnings, the massacres,
became woven in my soul
like a tenacious grapevine that won't let go.
I unearth the bloodroot
that runs through my family's psyche.
Was my father's madness conjured up
from some bitter vampire's brew
of pine needles, poison berries and blood libel?
Was he sickened from the spicy *lungen* stew
he found in *Little Transylvania* on West 96th Street?
The specter of Transylvania always threatened
to flood our house, shorten the glorious days of June.
Today, I pack my black knapsack
and travel to Transylvania
to explore the dark night of my soul.

II

There came a time when the risk to remain
tight in the bud was more painful
than the risk it took to blossom.
—Anais Nin

Invisible Star

I lived in an invisible galaxy
composed of dark matter
in the constellation Virgo,
swallowed by a black hole
in a fit of galactic cannibalism.
Unseen, I could be felt—
a triumph of gravity over matter.
Caught in a cyclone of desire,
I dreamed of a close encounter.

A Triangle of Unfinished Business

I am haunted by triangles.
Euclidean space eludes me.
But I live within its truths.
The sum of any two sides
of a triangle always exceeds
the length of the third side.
I grew up in a polygon
of lies, caught
between parents
at acute angles.
We refuted Pythagoras's theorem;
violated the law of cosines.
My mother obtuse/
my father, the circumventer.

Where Were We?

For David, Paul *and* Laurie Ellen

Where were we the winter
we celebrated Christmas?
That day we ran down
the stairs to mountains of toys,
inflated reindeer that outsized us,
the cranberry and gold tea set.
Far from our extended Jewish family,
the only witnesses, Mike,
the company chauffeur,
and our maid, Ernestine, hot pink
satin underwear hidden
underneath her starched uniform.
Where were we the day after?
When Mommy committed Daddy
to Hudson Valley State Mental Hospital
to be straitjacketed, shocked back to reality.
Where were we when she packed up
the house, moved back to Poughkeepsie,
to what she thought was the safety of her family?

WHAT HAPPENED TO *SHANA LEAH*?

Shana Leah, bat Nechamah
Pretty Leah, daughter of Nechamah.
What happened to that little curly
haired girl in the blue organdy dress,
straw bonnet, white gloves,
and black patent shoes?
Mommy, for what were you dressing me?
To whom did you deliver me?

Brush with Madness, Circa 1970

I have walked the edge,
toyed with madness,
but never succumbed
until the day I became Medusa,
my hair a wild mass of snakes.
A pearl of LSD opened the portal.
I stood naked in the shower.
A man I needed but did not want,
paced outside my door.
His lust pierced the keyhole.
Nipples erect, I felt both fear
and fury grow like fireweed.
Medusa played with my mind.
Perseus be damned, the vipers hissed.
Your death no matter, we'll still have power.
They took me to sword's edge.
I had already toyed with death.
The Dark Mother had promised me
oblivion, night rainbow of nothingness.
She midwifed what could not be born.
Nursed on her icy breasts, I grew strong.
She helped me push the serpents
back into my head
and brush away madness.

UNSPEAKABLE

Words spew forth,
sour and unspeakable
as my father in the night.
Insistent rhythms rock my body—
syncopated madness.
A wolf at my bedroom door.
Silence howled in the blackened night.
Disembodied, disemboweled,
fingers in my entrails,
seed seeped into my marrow,
pregnant with his shame.
Little deaths each time
he called me *cunt.*
Until I threatened suicide,
hung it around his neck.

TESHUVAH

Account and repent.

My father sits ragged, palsied,
a mere shard of himself,
the world slipping out of his grasp.
He who raged can barely whisper.
Once he cast a giant shadow,
flooded me with his fury.
His river of epithets wore me down.
On sunny days, a ringmaster of delight,
he enveloped me in excess.
When I was little, my mother sickened.
He took me as his concubine,
a slender white birch bent by his storms.
Sickened by blood cancer in my fifties,
my marrow muttered,
Only justice will bring you peace.
I kindled a burnt offering of my failings.
Like the priests of old, I donned
a *choshen mishpat*, a breastplate
of judgment, over my wounded heart.
I challenged this man, my father,
to answer for what he had done.
Account and repent.
Slice open your heart.
Let that be your legacy.

Silence his only reply.

Reparations

He thought he was through
with us long before his death.
No need for nasty reminders
of his lesser self.
Better to leave his largess
to the third wife,
modest though it was.
All that college money he took
when our mother threw him out
best forgotten.

A year after Jack died,
my brothers and I
each received $14.86
from his pension
for the three days
he lived in February, 2007.

Six years after his death,
I received a call from his third wife's son.
The Manhattan Insurance Group
sought the surviving offspring
of Jack and Norma Neustadt.
My brothers and I each received
two checks, one for $51.40,
the second for $56.20.
Not enough to pay my therapist.
The checks sit on my desk,
demanding attention.

CARRY-ON BAGGAGE

I carry my battered
duffel bag everywhere.
I wouldn't recognize
myself without it.
Nothing epic inside,
no craters carved
by roadside bombs.
It wasn't genocide or famine
that ravaged my life,
just my father's
nighttime incursions.
Some days the weight feels
oppressive as fog,
a ghostly mirage
that obscures my vision.
On others, it is a phantom
limb that still aches.
When old memories flood me,
fault lines appear
as familiar as my face.
I shove them in my duffel bag
and zip it shut.

WHAT IF?

After Stephen Levine's *There Are Words in Us*

There are words hidden
in my marrow that tremble.
Words that die before they are born,
that turn to ash before they are spoken.
Unsaid words that leave
footprints on my tongue.
What if my words burst into flame,
bittered my morning tea,
spilled into dawn's pale light?

PERVERSED PLEASURE

Still slung in his seventies,
my father posed for the camera
like Poseidon in a beige bikini.
No mortal could cause
the riptides and earthquakes
he unleashed.
Jack perversed pleasure,
discarded shattered shells.
At once, the eye of the storm,
and its turbulent machinations.

Confessions of a Sugar Addict

I have sucked sugar's tit
for sixty-four years,
hopped up
on white powder,
its jolt of energy
coursed through my veins.
I got hooked early,
my father the candy dealer.
Never satisfied with one Milky
Way Midnight, one Rocky Road,
one scoop of Death by Chocolate.
Today, despite my fear and longing,
I scream, *Enough!*

You Don't Understand

It's not enough to demonize him
even though he cast me
as Lolita in his grimy movie,
pierced my core,
made my body the enemy.
Though he hurt me,
I still loved him.
His fingerprints remain on my skin.
He sat at the head of the table,
bought me ice cream cones
and new dresses.

It's not enough to demonize him.
It won't help me be safe in my own skin.
Instead, let us call in the wise women
to burn sweet-grass, shed light,
heal the wounds, because
it's not enough to demonize him.

The cab driver dropped me
in front of a red brick house
on a raw November morning,
three years before *Roe v. Wade*.
He recognized the address.
Said I was lucky I got him—
Some cabbies hit girls up for cash.

Dr. Milan Vuitch wore brown alligator
shoes, a starched white shirt
with his initials monogrammed
on its French cuffs.
He glittered with gold.
I wanted to ask him,
*How many babies did you flush
down the toilet to afford this?*
But I couldn't.
My baby would soon join them.

Dr. Vuitch didn't give me anything for pain.
*You'll need to run out the back door
in case the cops come.*
He knew the drill—
he'd been arrested sixteen times.
Bleeding, I stumbled out,
spent the night in a run-down motel.
The next morning, I packed my knapsack
and took the train back to college.

BAD BOY OF NEUROBIOLOGY

That dirt road on the outskirts
of Rochester, your black Harley,
my arms around your chest,
breasts hugging your back
as we tested gravity with every curve.
The scent of clovered afternoons
as we tangled in the grass,
slender ribbons of your
hair in my mouth.
You monkeyed around
with hamsters and rats.
Picked apart brains,
dissected hearts.
Plagiarized love poems
from Wallace Stevens.

You never loved me.
I bruised like a peach
when you said, *no.*
Destroyed the fruit we had sown
in that brick house in Baltimore.
Forty years later, you plucked
me out of the orchard of oblivion,
put me under your microscope,
then discarded me again.

I Did Not Set Out to Be Cruel

I just wanted to
help this man I did not love.
He asked me to stay as
long as it took him to mend.
Something about his impotence
fascinated me.
Perhaps my childhood
fantasy that my father
would become powerless.
At first, I would lay bare
my breasts, open my arms,
never ask him to enter.
Week after week, we would
sit in the therapist's office.
Then return to his apartment
to the twin bed with steel posts
that barely contained
his mute body and my lies.
I did not set out to be cruel.
I could not mend myself,
let alone this man I did not love.
No longer a child, this time
I fled the tangled lies.

May It Please the Court

Oyez, oyez, oyez
chants the court crier.
All rise as seven judges
robed in black file
into the majestic chamber.
Row upon row
of appellate advocates
wait their turn.

I am turned out
in a black suit
with a forties flare-
a nod to Lauren Bacall.
Dressed in black patent
pumps, sheer black hose,
an extra pair stuffed
in my briefcase,
just enough gold to glint.

Facts honed with a lathe,
legal principles loaded
like a spring gun,
only fifteen minutes
to press my client's case.
Years of anger and anguish
summarized in Times Roman
font on recycled white paper,
bound by Rules of Court.

Seven judges robed in black
pound me with questions.
I dodge, deflect, then
swing with white gloves.
The red light blinks.
Your time is up counselor.

Months later,
the edict is issued,
precedent set.
Plaintiff and defendant
pressed into law books
like dried flowers.

FIRST-BORN

The doctors said there was less than a ten percent chance he would survive.

He didn't want to be a miracle boy—
just himself, though taller.
He didn't want to be my *Machu Picchu*,
not even Matthew, my gift from God.
Drawing boundaries,
he staked his claim in the world.
My name is Matt.
He didn't want a mother
with a satchel of worries,
who wove stories from falling stars.
He wanted to explore outer space,
to float without the gravity
of a mother's love.
He dreamed himself
a paleontologist at four—
hungered for facts
set in ancient bone.
Surgeon in the making,
he is still a man of facts,
though softened
by love and marriage.
Now that he is a father,
I wonder what stories he will weave.

Thank You, Tupac

I was ready for a simple love, though no love is simple.
Nothing prepared me for the messiness of mothering.
Adolescent sons who needed me strong and confident
found me confused, weighed down with worry.
Our suburban home was overtaken by rappers
with bling bling. Rancorous rhythms rang out.
Tupac Shakur, cult king of rap, issued a challenge,
his angry bird in my face. They were dangerous times.
It was only hope—like the rising sun—
that kept me going as I waited for havoc to unfold.
Ironically it was Tupac who brought
love and a peace of sorts to our home.
His rap of thanks to his mama inspired Benjamin
to sing his own song of the street.
Knowing my doubts, he soothed my soul.
May you be by my side when my children are born
for your presence will make their lives richer.
Benjamin's song healed my heart.
When he called the next day
burdened by midnight blues,
I sang his hymn of faith.
Thank you, Tupac.

The Sacrament of Sushi

I sit alone at the sushi bar.
My son, now a chef,
serves me *kani sunomono*,
hairy crab from Hokkaido,
fashioned as a flower,
crowned with chrysanthemum.
Moments later, Benjamin
comes bearing *akamutsu*,
a strand of snapper
laid upon a sliver of daikon
adorned with shiso flowers.
I savor the edible haiku.
I imagine my father
beside me, resurrected.
He claims Benjamin
as his own, though he
barely knew him.
He seeks redemption
from Benjamin's knife-worn hands.
Tastes his seasoning
in Benjamin's passion.
I wrestle with this gluttonous ghost.
Remember the bacchanalia of his life.
Benjamin reappears with *katsuo dashi*,
a delicate broth of golden mushrooms
cradled in a wooden vessel,
slender as sea shell. I take
the wooden chalice,

and chant *Kaddish* again.
My son offers me
persimmon, plucked from Japan,
its orange flesh iced sweet.
We share the sacrament of sushi.

BITTER GREENS

Benjamin didn't have a chance—
cooking was his inheritance.
At eight he was seduced
by dining out with Grandpa Jack
at a posh club in Palm Beach.
Jack knew the chef.
He towered over Benjamin
in his white toque
and monogrammed chef's jacket
with nary a stain.
The chef came to woo them
after sending an *amuse-bouché*.
As Benjamin grew, cooking
became a sacred calling,
a priesthood. He took vows,
sacrificed to serve under masters—
Robuchon, Morimoto, Masa.
He savored the feel
of the knife as he slashed
through saffron flesh
of Alaskan salmon.
Happily beheaded ducks,
coveted their feet for stock,
seared their breasts
to rosy perfection.
Drawn to the austere
beauty of the East,
he prepared sea creatures

adorned with shiso flowers.
But the pearl began
to lose its luster.

Night after night
Benjamin labors on the line,
hands skewered by sharp knives,
arms mottled with burns,
bones spurred from slicing.
There is ferment in his kitchen,
chafing dishes of resentment.
Stripped of his spices,
Benjamin is bittered green.
He makes little more
than minimum wage,
no benefits save family meal.
He's deboned and deglazed.
His hands ache, akin
to great-grandparents
who labored in sweatshops
a century ago.

The Salt Wars, Circa 2010

Trade routes…were established, alliances built, empires
secured, and revolutions provoked all for something that fills
the ocean, [and] bubbles up from springs…
—Mark Kurlansky, *Salt: A World History*

We eye each other warily,
no longer certain of the steps
in this lifelong dance of mother and son.
He brash, I bedeviled in this covenant of salt.
Salt the latest skirmish, rife with rocky deposits,
both preserver and provocateur.
For my son, Benjamin, salt is the Holy Grail.
Salting a rite of sanctification.
He creates crystalline castles
with fleur de sel from Provence.
Sprinkles holy bread with salt
blackened in Hawaiian volcanoes.
Coaxes the scarlet flesh of heirloom tomatoes
to give up their souls for our pleasure.
Bathes turbot in brine until it bursts
forth like the evening star.
Unrefined, I season our food
with worried grains.
When I take up Benjamin's salty challenge,
I recall how we dip greens in salt
to remember our ancestors' tears.
I remember blessing my sons,
Become the salt of the earth.

WATER IS MY TEMPLE

Shechinah represents the feminine presence of God.

I need no edifice
to seek *Shechinah's* glory,
for water is my Temple.
Shechinah's omnipotence
revealed in every drop.
Water's warm cascades
bring me to life;
I linger in its luminosity.
I drink from Miriam's Cup,
satisfy thirst on sacred fare,
for water is my Temple.
I surrender shame,
only radiance remains.
I dive joyously for divine sparks,
a mermaid in its depths.
Stripped bare in the *Mikveh*,
I float in living waters,
soak in *Shechinah's* compassion.
Like the new moon
I ripen to fullness,
for water is my Temple.

III

There is a brokenness out of which comes the unbroken,
a shatteredness out of which blooms the unshatterable.
—Rashani

Resurrection

The crystal ball sparkled at Times Square
as we toasted the New Year.
My husband collapsed at countdown.
At ten, the left side of his body crumpled.
By nine, he lost consciousness.
At eight, the restaurant was silent.
By seven, we called 911.
At six, he was revived.
By five, he rose with slurred speech.
At four, he staggered out on a friend's arm.
By three, an ambulance was summoned.
At two, we waited in the frigid air.
An ancient ambulance arrived at one.
The ball dropped as we bounced
down back roads to Ellis Hospital.
Transferred to gurney,
IV started, monitor on,
Gary waited in a blue gown.
Over half-hearted protest,
he was admitted,
his interior scanned and probed.
No trace left in his brain or heart
that tests could measure.
Only a faint, Dr. Brooks said.
Nothing showed,
but nothing is the same.

TURNING POINT

To our first grandson who was born on March 14, 2012

We have not wintered well.
The weeping willow choked on its roots,
Austrian pines felled by fungus,
weeping cherry trees succumbed to cold.
Tree by tree our family has withered.
Each year fewer and fewer tulips
make their way to the sun.

But the buds on the magnolia
tree are about to burst.
They will swirl around in white
skirts, then fall, still dancing.
The daffodils are blazing in their bonnets.
Tender green shoots turn their faces to the sun.
We open our arms like blossoms,
greet Mason with joy.

CHILD OF MY CHILD

Baptized with sunlight,
you birth new shoots,
cast me in your puddled joy.
Renew my faith in the miracle
of in and out and in again.
Disarmed, I fall
through your rabbit hole,
nourished by your delight.

After My Husband Has Seen 25 Patients

Be patient—
let the smoke clear.
Follow the trail
of animal crackers.
Admire him in his own habitat
as he falls asleep
watching the golf channel,
medical journal by his side.

BLOOD OFFERING

I offer up 27 vials of blood,
four teaspoons of marrow,
two slices of bone.
Seek revelation
in the Book of Numbers,
life revealed in counts.

There is no abacus. No burning
bush. No stone tablet
to help me find my way.
Just my still, small voice.

Doctors contemplate chemical warfare.
Calculate the innocents
who must be sacrificed.
I wait in the shadows.

THE WAITING ROOM

We sit like riders
on the subway, eyes averted.
There is only one reason to be
at Dana-Farber Cancer Institute.
Paper bracelets on our wrists announce:
This is the one with cancer.

A raven haired woman wears
a black sweater with blood-
orange embroidery.
Still sturdy, with an iron heart,
not hardened, but rusty.
Voice raised, eyebrows arched,
she harangues her husband in Russian.

Unlike the frail patients—
wasted, eyes vacant,
taste for living sapped.
Masks and gloves
offer little protection.
Their parents, children, lovers
try to keep them afloat.
Those of us who are sick
but still feisty
draw lines in the sand.

Listen, Please Listen

Sweet crimson and golden marrow,
birthplace of my blood,
let light suffuse your spongy core.
Call upon Kali to banish the invaders
who have infiltrated my bones.
Nurture the tender chrysalis
of each stem cell so it can
bloom into a butterfly.
Nourish the poets of red
who bring breath to my body.
Strengthen the white-coated warriors
who defend me from harm.
Be open to miracles.

Death's Seduction

Death has seduced me.
Unwittingly I flirt
with an untimely demise.
Imagine joining my mother and sister.
But then, I recall
Death's cruel wrath,
the hunger of unfulfilled desire,
the emptiness of sacred
vessels left behind.
Death's startling kiss
has sharpened my vision.
I savor the messy stew of my life.

Around the Corner

I feel my thin shell,
the fragile yoke inside,
as I trudge down Rosendale Road.
Its lanes leave little room for ramblers.
Slender white lines weave
a foot or two from the edge—
only inches from hurtling SUV's.

Summer is on its last legs.
A skunk lies dead,
his feet reach toward the sky.
No evidence of cataclysm
colors his body.
Nature's rites have begun;
his life celebrated by flies.
No other mourners in sight.
The harsh chorus
of crows yet to arrive.

I have driven down this road
a thousand times,
but never felt the brute force,
never noticed the hidden
drive that only appears to those
who walk close to the earth.

Stringing Beads at Gilda's Club

It seems so simple
to string beads
on steel wire.
But when you sit
among the dying,
it becomes something else.
Almost like breathing
in and out
until there is only silence.
To bead among the dying
is to be pierced to the core.
You string out lives
bead by bead,
a rosary of prayer.

The Cartographer

Lost in a desert,
the parchment lies bare,
journey uncharted.
No waywiser to take measure.
No legend to interpret the tale.
I need a wayfinder
to get my bearings.
Even without a compass,
I sense true north ahead,
though I cannot imagine
the topography of the land.

Night Sounds, Circa 2003

I awake grasping for breath,
my cough the only chorus in the night.
I make my way down darkened stairs,
a nebulizer awaits.
My mother's ghost greets me,
bemoaning her breathless legacy.

Thank You

I have never liked mice.
They burrow into our homes,
multiply like pomegranate seeds,
taint our food.
It is hard to thank them for their sacrifice.
Thousands have lost their lives
fighting cancer.
They did not enlist in this war.
They were not happy to die.
Their protein molecules
carry monoclonal antibodies
that kill my cancer cells.
I feel their protest
in my joints and my belly,
my liver and my lungs.

Memento Mori

The unreadiness is all we have,
no matter how close
that final breath.
No matter what,
that silence will startle—
will take our breath away.

LUNAR ECLIPSE

The full moon called
from the rear-view mirror
as we made our way home.
It cast an ethereal glow
to the evening sky.
Both cranky,
our conversation mean-spirited,
my husband chided,
You are frail,
hoping to slow me down.
Later that night,
fear pierced my dreams.
The moon summoned me.
I bathed in its light
until its topaz tones darkened,
hidden by an ebony veil.
Under its dark spell,
I drew fear's face
and befriended her.

IV

Sanctity is not a paradise but a paradox.

—Rabbi Joseph Soloveitchik

A Remembrance of Beauty

In memory of Ruth St. Denis *who danced through her 80's*

She slips into the studio at sunrise,
coaxing her body out of its ancient shell
as she dances to the strains of Satie.
Her faint movements hint of grandeur.
A time when her gossamer body
was supple as clay, able to bring forth
oceans of possibility, canyons of desire.
Hidden in the shadows,
her husband watches.
He sees a leap in each measured step,
a pirouette in every slight turn.
He prays her body remembers
the beauty his eyes still see.

SANDHOGS

*Sandhog is a slang term for a construction worker who
excavates underwater tunnels.*

The Hudson River refuses
to give up its secrets today.
No reflections from above,
no hint of what lies hidden.
Even the clouds are veiled.
But shadows won't be denied.
They cast themselves on muddled
waters, tarnish the sun's polished eye.
I leave the safety of the highway,
drive into the Lincoln Tunnel.
Hear the river cry for the sandhogs
coffined in its depths.

REFLECTION

I want to feel my connection to the squirrel
who stands in prayer on my front lawn,
the Japanese maple dressed in crimson
outside my window, even the flood waters
rising at my backdoor. I want to cover
myself with a blanket of leaves,
run my fingers through rippled water
without need to steer my canoe.
I long to let the river take me
to an estuary bursting
with bulrushes and birds.

UNDER COVER OF NIGHT

I dig grapple hooks
into the rocky ledge,
unable to sling rope
to the next out-cropping.
I live as if the ledge
were my summit.
Fleeing daylight,
I seek refuge in dark caves.
Under cover of night,
I dream of swooping down
past fertile fields
lush with honeysuckle
into shimmering seas,
floating light
as a jellyfish.

LISTEN

Lines from *18 Stethoscopes, One Heart Murmur and Many
Missed Connections* by Madeline Drexler, *New York Times,*
Science Section, 3/1/2011

Listen to the muffled cadence
of the marching band—
the invisible touchstone
that flutters and skips,
thunks and whooshes,
with telltale pitches and tempos.

Part artist's model,
part one night stand,
I sit in my open-stringed
green and blue gown, and say,
It wasn't until the 18th student
that someone bothered to ask my name.

It Must Be Hard to Be an Icon

The Dalai Lama sits on stage
at the Palace Theater.
Magnified on a large screen,
he scratches his head and chin,
takes off his oxfords,
pulls up his brown socks,
sits cross-legged
on an easy chair.
He squints at the blinding
spotlights, tugs at his maroon robe,
and pulls out a maroon visor.
He begins with a confession.
*I am not a healer. If I were, I wouldn't
have needed gallbladder surgery.*
The theater resounds with laughter.
*My life hasn't been happy since I was ousted
from my homeland decades ago.*
Somehow this man, His Holiness,
the fourth Dalai Lama,
crowned as a toddler,
finds a way to giggle in exile.
I listen for pearls of wisdom
to string like prayer beads,
but it is the lotus of his laughter
I carry home.

Nestled in the Shade of the Elder Tree

Two women rest on a wooden bench
on the banks of the Mohawk River.
One sits in the sun, her face
a map of many journeys.
The other, face untraveled,
rests her head on the elder's lap.
The grandmother strokes
her granddaughter's downy arms
over and over,
an endless river of love.

BEADS OF WONDER

Sometimes the universe is too big.
We conquer it bit by bit,
unearth beads buried deep in the earth.
When I am adrift, I find my ground
in turquoise carved in the pueblos of New Mexico,
silver beads shaped by hill tribes in Thailand,
translucent glass blown in Murano,
crystals fashioned in Czechoslovakia.
Beads offer me pearls of procrastination,
malas of meditation.
I join them in colorful communion.
When a necklace takes shape,
I know the beads will outlive me.

RECURRENCE

If only it were a perseveration,
a phantom of my opera,
an aria I can't get out of my head.
But the tremolo is real—
the tenor gone awry.
There is no bel canto. No sparkling
soprano lifts me to my feet.
I know the libretto.
The impresario has called for a *calando*.
I demand an encore,
sung with fortissimo.

WAITING ROOM II: THE AMYLOID CLINIC

I sit alone in the waiting room
next to Arthur who needs a new heart.
A woman with two young daughters
suggests I rent a place at Furnished Quarters
across the street from the Christian
Science Monitor Building
if I need a stem cell transplant.
I tell everyone I'll hire a handsome young man
to care for me. Phyllis is worried.
She warns me to hire a woman.
I don't think a handsome young man
will take care of you.
Will she understand
my preference for a gay man
with a sense of humor?
I don't know my audience well enough.
It's only our second day together
as we wait to be called
for our next test or appointment.
My companions talk
about their heart, kidney,
and stem cell transplants,
their years of chemotherapy.
I imagine family photos without me.
But then I hear my grandson's
infectious laughter and I am
determined to remain.

IMMERSION

Inspired by Channing Lefebvre's painting, *Autumn Evening*

Warmed by saffron sun,
I sink in golden earth
worn to silk.
Wade in still waters,
enveloped in the cool,
uncurled blue.
Creature of the sea,
I glide along the surface,
stroke by stroke.
Then emerge senses sated.

SILENCE

Enter the sanctuary
of her dark womb.
Listen to your heart
pulse in the red sea.
What seems like a watery
tomb will open.
Greet your shadow
like a friend, words unspoken.

Awash with Images

Nothing is safe from my scissors.
I ravish *Architectural Digest, Art and Antiques,*
National Geographic, The New York Times.
I hear my husband call for the
Arts Section of *The Sunday Times.*
Too late, my dear.
I cut what catches me,
garish, grisly or sublime.
Lemurs, lions, ladies-in-waiting,
owls, monkeys, mummies, and men.
I fuse images for reasons
that elude me.
Yet, when I let the images speak,
they read me like tarot.

PIECE BY PIECE

Our imagination can probe the heights of Spirit and the
depths of Soul, traveling often on the wings of images.
—Seema B. Frost

When I am lost
in splintered shells of myself,
ephemera lead me home.
My scissors hone my vision.
I find revelation in images.
I piece myself
together with glue.
Annoint handmade papers
with iridescent paints and pastels,
facet them with found objects.
My collages sing to me
of connection, paradox
and mystery.
Their dark melodies reveal
what cannot be discerned
by words alone.

I Want to Live

in saffron light,
to step into the warmth
until it swells inside me
like the harvest moon.
I want to live in the space
between drum beats,
my heart resonating
like taut deer skin,
its animal heart
beating with mine.

Forgiveness

I bundle my burdens,
place them on the altar,
burn them with sage.
I release my father
to his own reckoning.
Now free, I can lie
in a child's pose
in sweet surrender.

Symphony of Blues

Inspired by a still life painted by Dorothy Englander

Aquamarine seeps into azure.
Cerulean slides into cobalt.
Sky blue flows into sapphire,
with a hint of smoke and sea.
Two flowered vases stand at center stage.
One, tall and stately, is adorned
with white lilies and blue lupines.
Though the second vase is empty,
it flowers of its own beauty.
Its ample figure is florid;
it flaunts a bit of raucous red
among the muted blossoms.
Even the walls sing of flowers.
I flourish in this symphony of blues.

Flower of a Thousand Petals

White lotus,
flower of a thousand petals,
let me enter your womb.
Unfold your wings,
reveal your golden seeds,
fill me with your wisdom.
Bloom of mystery,
take me beyond the veil
to the time before time.

Aftermath

Brittle, my body bears
the brunt of years of treatment.
I can no longer digest my life.
While I rejoice in my remission,
I still need chemotherapy
to keep cancer and amyloidosis at bay.
Though modern medicine is my lifeline,
I seek the wisdom of shamans and starkeepers.
It is they who infuse me with luminosity,
who inspire me to live lightly,
fully present, but not quite of this world.

The Seed Keepers

It was the Seed Keepers
who saved me,
reminded me who I was,
sang me back to life
with ancient songs.
Purified by rain,
I grow fertile again.
Deeply rooted
in rich black loam,
my heirloom seeds
bear fruit.

Bearing Fruit

Sometimes truth
has sharp edges
that pierce my skin.
The lullaby of lies I've sung,
a hand-me-down coat
that no longer fits.
Sometimes truth bubbles up
like a spring. Bloody water
no white wash can clean.
Then it is time to burst
like a pomegranate
and spill my ruby seeds.
Only then can I reclaim
the sun's kiss and let the juice
of blood oranges flow
from my lips.

Leslie B. Neustadt was born in Poughkeepsie, New York. She received her B.A. in History from the University of Rochester and her J.D. from Temple University School of Law in 1976. A former Assistant Attorney General for the state of New York, she retired from that office following a long and rewarding career. She began writing in the warm embrace of womanwords, a peer writing group founded by Marilyn Day in the Capital Region of New York.

A member of the International Women's Writing Guild and the Hudson Valley Writers Guild, Leslie created an award winning Community of Jewish Writers reading series in the Capital Region. Pursuing a wide range of expressive arts and holistic practices as part of her healing journey, her work is illuminated by her Jewish background. Her poems explore the challenges she's faced living with serious health problems including a rare form of incurable blood cancer and amyloidosis, as well as other chronic illnesses. She writes openly about her experiences as an incest survivor.

Her poems and essays have appeared in a variety of literary journals and publications including *Akros Review, Cure, Cylamens and Swords, Found Poetry Review, Jewish Women's Literary Annual, Mused: BellaOnline Literary Review, Poetica,* and *Workers Write: Tales from the Courtroom*. She has been published in several anthologies including *peer glass* (Hudson Valley Writers Guild), *Mentor's Bouquet* (Finishing Line Press), *The Bloomsbury Anthology of Contemporary Jewish American Poetry* (Bloomsbury Press), and the forthcoming anthology *Veils, Halos and Shackles: International Poetry on the Abuse and Oppression of Women*.

She continues to find inspiration and solace through her writing and artwork, giving voice to her experiences as a woman, daughter, wife, mother, patient and survivor. About Leslie's writing, author Natalie Reid has said, "Leslie Neustadt is a gift. Her raw-boned, unvarnished humanity and quest for forgiveness—of both herself and others—resonate throughout the journey on which she takes us. Her poems, at once delicate and compelling, teach us to 'surrender shame' and 'sense true north' in the unmapped territories of our lives."

Leslie lives with her husband, Dr. Gary Kronick, in Niskayuna, New York. They are the parents of two adult sons, and are proud grandparents.

Made in the USA
Charleston, SC
30 April 2014